BRITAIN IN OLD PHOTOGRAPHS

AROUND HELSTON

A superb study of fishing luggers in the outer harbour at Porthleven by the Helston photographer A.H. Hawke. Hawke must have been pleased with it because it is printed to a far higher standard than his run-of-the-mill cards, as later pictures will show. The lifeboat house is at the top left.

BRITAIN IN OLD PHOTOGRAPHS

AROUND HELSTON

PETER Q. TRELOAR

ALAN SUTTON PUBLISHING LIMITED

Alan Sutton Publishing Limited
Phoenix Mill · Far Thrupp · Stroud
Gloucestershire · GL5 2BU

First published 1995

Copyright © Peter Q. Treloar, 1995

Cover photographs: (front) looking down
Coinage Street, Helston, *c.* 1950; (back) the
Helston Furry Dance – soldiers join in an
informal dance at about the time of the First
World War.

British Library Cataloguing in Publication Data.
A catalogue record for this book is available from
the British Library.

ISBN 0-7509-0876-9

Typeset in 9/10 Sabon.
Typesetting and origination by
Alan Sutton Publishing Limited.
Printed in Great Britain by
Ebenezer Baylis, Worcester.

Contents

	Introduction	7
1.	The Heart of Helston	9
2.	The Rest of Helston	21
3.	Porthleven	31
4.	The Loe to Polurrian	41
5.	Mullion to Kynance	55
6.	The Lizard	73
7.	Cadgwith to Coverack	89
8.	Around the Helford	105
9.	Flora Day	115
	Acknowledgements	126

Helston is best known for the Furry Dance, held on or near 8 May each year. Here is a typical scene of the late fifties with the Midday Dance coming down Church Street from its starting point in the Guildhall at the top. The leading gentleman is Mr Jack Gilbert.

Introduction

A few years ago I prepared the book in the 'In Old Photographs' series relating to Calne in Wiltshire where I now live. Alan Sutton Publishing asked if I would write a sequel but I had to decline for lack of material. However, I mentioned that I had a considerable collection of Cornish photographs and was delighted to learn that a book had yet to be prepared covering my home town of Helston. Thus I was commissioned to compile the book covering Helston and Meneage. I was born at Praa Sands but my parents came from Helston and I spent much time with my grandmother Mrs Eddy (whom many will remember as a primary school teacher) while attending her school in Penrose Road, so Helston was indeed my home town.

This book is unusual in the 'In Old Photographs' series in that it is illustrated entirely with postcards. This has proved possible because the Helston area attracted many fine photographers on account of its physical beauty and the ready sale to tourists, especially in the heyday of the postcard in the period from 1900 to 1914. While the cards naturally include a high proportion of landscape scenes, there are many showing local people, activities and events; coverage of the Furry Dance is almost overwhelming.

There is little coverage of inland Meneage as the settlements are predominantly coastal, originally because of fishing and shipping activities and later, tourism. However, Helston itself is a few miles inland, as are some of the villages like St Keverne and Manaccan. Helston lies at the neck of the peninsula which stretches out to England's southern extremity at Lizard Point, bounded by Mount's Bay to the west, the Channel round the Point to the east and the Helford River cutting deep inland to Gweek on the north. Helston was the natural focus and centre for this area, known from medieval times as Meneage but more commonly referred to as The Lizard nowadays.

Helston is an ancient town. Its earliest charter was granted by King John in 1201. It has had an interesting history and is famous world-wide as the home of the Furry Dance. It is perhaps under-rated as an attractive town in its own right. How many towns can show such a group of comparatively unspoiled traditional thoroughfares as Coinagehall, Meneage, Church and Cross Streets? Then there are minor delights like the kennels and the back lanes. The Lizard also may be considered neglected in comparison with the better-known Land's End peninsula but many would argue that with its serpentine cliffs, wild Goonhilly Downs, unique Loe Bar, pretty fishing coves and the contrasting lushness of the Helford, it has scenery of a character and variety unmatched in Cornwall. I hope this book will highlight the rare and distinctive qualities of the area.

The dramatic serpentine cliffs of The Lizard peninsula are one of the great features of the area and they contain a number of impressive caves. This one at The Lizard is known as Dolor Hugo, *hugo* or *ogo* being Cornish for cave. (Edwardian card, Peacock Series.)

THE HEART OF
HELSTON

An early Argall's Series card of the Grylls Monument at the bottom of Coinagehall Street.
The man's dirty clothing and the ladder suggest that he and the boy may have been a chimney-
sweeping team.

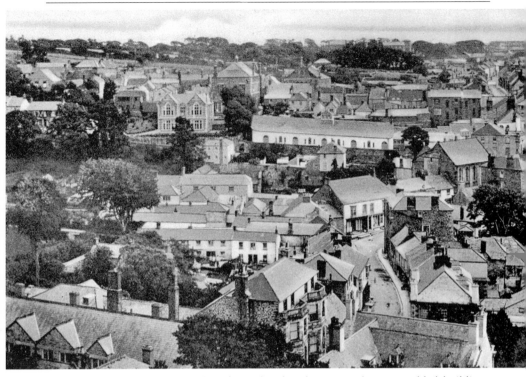

A view of the central area, taken from the church tower. The twin-gabled building, facing left of centre, started life as the Passmore Edwards Science and Art School and was later incorporated into the County School, which opened in 1905. Behind it is the Godolphin Hall and to its right the Market House. The Willows is in the centre foreground with Church Street leading from it past the United Methodist church to the Guildhall near the top right. (A Peacock Brand card bearing the name of Griffiths & Leaver, publishers, Helston.)

The crossroads at the centre of Helston, the top of Coinagehall Street leading into Wendron Street and Meneage Street turning off to the right opposite the then Cornish Bank, now Lloyds. This side of the Guildhall, Church Street drops away down the hill. The granite-built Guildhall, originally the Corn Exchange, in severely classical style, dates from 1839. The shop below it was already C. Wakeham, Chemist. This photograph must have been taken well before the First World War although it was not posted until 1917.

Looking down Coinagehall Street from opposite the Guildhall in early post-Second World War days. Apart from the tarmac and the cars, not much has changed in comparison with the next picture. Wakeham's Chemists is still there. (Frith's Series.)

Coinagehall Street in Edwardian times, depicted on an Argall's Series card. The horse buses were a great feature of the Helston scene before the introduction of motor buses from 1903 onwards. As well as the one on the right (bearing the name T.M. James on its back door) at least one more is standing at right angles to the street further down. They served mainly the Meneage peninsula and are entertainingly described in A.S. Oates's *Around Helston In The Old Days*.

This card, posted to France in 1921, depicts a meet of the hounds at the bottom of Coinagehall Street with the Grylls Monument beyond. The thatched building at the left is the Blue Anchor Inn, still famous for its home-brewed 'Spingo' ales.

The south side of Coinagehall Street in evening sunshine, photographed by A.H. Hawke in about 1930. This study highlights the quality and character of the street, which is one of the finest in Cornwall to this day. As well as the homogeneous yet varied buildings, the kennels of running water down each side are a most attractive and unusual feature. It is very regrettable that the granite-faced building right of centre was in post-war years replaced by the present characterless and out-of-scale post office. The building originated in the eighteenth century as the town house of the Trevenen family of Bonython (Oates, p. 65). It later became Simpson's Garage, as shown in the photograph, and even in that guise retained characteristic features, such as an oval staircase, which I remember from childhood parties. The street acquired its name from the Coinage Hall which once stood in the wide lower part of the street above the site of the Grylls Monument. From about the twelfth century until 1837, tin production was under royal control and tin had to be produced for testing and taxing at one of the five Cornish coinage towns. Pending the infrequent coinages, tin was stored in the Coinage Hall and there it was eventually assayed and, if pure, stamped. Until the Reformation the Coinage Hall was the fourteenth-century Chapel of Our Lady, the name of which has now passed to Lady Street (Toy, pp. 146–8 and 411–14).

An early Valentine card of the Wesleyan chapel or church in Coinagehall Street. The building now known as the Epworth Hall behind it was built in about 1795 and replaced by this church in 1888, as recorded in the central stone of the pediment. It was constructed by local builder W.J. Winn and, with the site, cost £5,000.

The very typically Methodist interior of the church, with its pine pews and gallery and the prominent preacher's pulpit with organ behind. The building was declared unsafe in 1988 (its centenary) and subsequently completely restructured. A floor has been inserted into the area shown, creating a worship room seating 250 on the first floor, while a hall, Sunday School suite and other ancillary rooms are situated on the ground floor. The work cost £360,000 and the church was reopened in March 1995.

A fine real-photo card by E.A. Bragg & Co., Illogan, depicting Flora Day. The photograph was probably taken in 1907 but the date is indecipherable. An expectant crowd is assembled on the Bowling Green in front of the Grylls Monument. The Grylls family, sometime of Bosahan, was very prominent in borough affairs in the late eighteenth and nineteenth centuries. Two brothers, Richard Gerveys Grylls and Thomas Grylls, were between them twelve times mayor. Thomas's sons Humphrey Millett and Glynn were, in all, eleven times mayor. The monument was erected in memory of Humphrey Millett Grylls, 1789–1834. He was particularly popular because of his efforts to keep the great Wheal Vor copper mine open (Toy, pp. 593–4; Oates, p. 64). The monument was built by Thomas Eva of Helston. The Bowling Green is the reputed site of Helston's medieval castle (Toy, p. 398–9).

Flora Day, 1907. The Grylls Monument is in the background, although the ceremony is taking place on the Coinagehall Street side. The caption states that the Lord Mayor is receiving the children's contributions for the Crippled Children's Fund. Sir William Purdie Treloar was Lord Mayor of London in 1906–7. It is often said that he was a Helstonian but one has to go back to his grandfather William, born at Wendron in 1768, to find his local roots. William's son Thomas was born at Portishead near Bristol in 1818 and became the owner of a coconut fibre business which developed into the Treloar & Son Carpet Co. of Ludgate Hill, London. From that base his son William Purdie (born 1843) entered City politics and in due course became Lord Mayor. Best-known for his concern for crippled children, he established the fund being augmented here. He later established the Lord Mayor Treloar Cripples' Hospital and College at Alton, Hants. He was knighted in 1900 and made Baronet in 1907 shortly before his visit. He died in 1923. (Details from the remarkable *Treloar Genealogy* by O.L. Treloar, Utah, *c.* 1962.)

A card by Jarrold looking up Meneage Street, taken soon after the Second World War and showing how the street retained its eighteenth- and nineteenth-century character.

A much earlier Frith card, posted in 1903, looking in the opposite direction down Meneage Street.

A Frith card showing the same view, with a Second World War army truck approaching. Though it dates from the early post-war period the only noticeable change, apart from the vehicles, is Eddy's Odeon-style shopfront of the thirties. While a fine example of its genre, it is an unfortunate disfigurement of the Georgian façade seen in the last picture.

The middle part of Meneage Street at the beginning of this century depicted in an Argall's Series card with the characteristic 'extras' deployed. The street then had kennels which have since been hidden to make more space for traffic. The drapers on the left must have been the late lamented B. Thomas's. The building just visible at the right (the Horse & Jockey Inn) has probably been twice renewed to create the present modern shop unit.

The top end of Meneage Street at about the same time as the picture on p. 19, but with rather more skilfully posed extras. There are running kennels on both sides of the carriageway. The thatched cottage to the left was soon after replaced by a double shop/house building which still carries the 1703 building stone of the cottage as well as its own 1913 date. The posters on the cottage advertise shipping lines such as Union Castle, Cunard and Allan Line (for Canada), reminders of the massive emigration from Cornwall which followed the mine closures of the second half of the nineteenth century. (Eddy & Son's Series.)

THE REST OF HELSTON

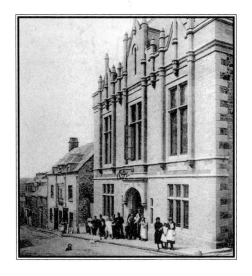

An early Frith card of the Godolphin Hall in Wendron Street, posted in January 1903.

The Methodist Church became prone to division in the nineteenth century with the result that both the Bible Christians and the Wesleyan Methodist Association established separate chapels in the town. In 1838 the construction of the Market House and Penrose Road provided a corner site on which a brewery previously stood. The Association built its new church there, with chapel above and schoolroom in the basement below. The Association, by then the United Methodist Free Church, joined the general reunification of the Methodist Church in 1932 but congregations did not unite at once. This chapel was demolished, having deteriorated dangerously, quite recently. This splendid Hawke photo card was posted in 1913, and W.F. Ivey has identified the subject as a Convention of Local Preachers. (See Toy, pp. 351–3.)

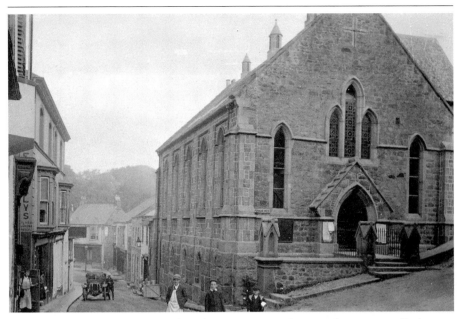

The Free Church chapel, pictured in this anonymous photo card, was generally known as 'The Little Ship', for reasons unknown to the author. On the left is a glimpse of Church Street in Edwardian times, the early car (reg. no. L126, perhaps an MMC Tonneau) indicating the first years of this century.

Although just around the corner from the scene above and dating from the same period, there are no motor vehicles in this view of Church Street. The New Inn on the right bears the name of licensee E. Lancastle. Published by Stengel & Co., London, it was, like many contemporary cards, printed in Germany.

In the eighteenth century St Michael's Church became ruinous and was replaced by the present building. The cost was borne by the 2nd Earl of Godolphin. The pace of building was leisurely, from 1756 to 1761, during which time the Guildhall had to be used for worship. This Wrench Series view, posted in 1903, shows the approach up from Church Street. The tower is 103 feet high and contains eight bells, six originating in 1767 (gifted by the same Earl of Godolphin, who had died in 1766, ending the male line) and two in 1904. The granite of which the church is built came from Tregonning Hill.

The interior of St Michael's Church on a Valentine card. The galleries were inserted in the nineteenth century to accommodate increasing congregations. The fine chandelier is inscribed 'This branch, together with the compleat building of the church and chancel, is the sole gift and benefaction of the Right Honourable the Earl of Godolphin, bestowed on this Borough, A.D. 1763.' The pulpit, of Bath stone, was erected in 1899 (Toy, chapter XXI).

Although well known, this splendid Frith view of Wendron Street early this century could hardly be omitted from a survey of the town. Not much has changed on the left side, apart from the kennel having disappeared, but the cottages on the right have given way to the County School playground. Godolphin Hall is just visible in the background on the left side of the street.

Further down Wendron Street in the same era. Godolphin Hall, centre left, is perhaps partly on the site of the original Helston Grammar School, of which one building survives to the rear right of the hall. The school was famous in the first half of the nineteenth century, when Derwent Coleridge, son of the poet, was headmaster, Revd C.A. Johns who wrote 'Flowers of the Field' was assistant, and Charles Kingsley, best known as author of *The Water Babies*, was a pupil. (Argall's Series.)

The middle part of Godolphin Road, again early this century, with posed delivery cart and Lugg's Temperance Hotel to the left. Under a different name, the building was the same when I passed it every day as a schoolboy in the forties. The anonymous card was posted to Kentish Town in 1907: 'we arrived here quite safe on Wednesday night we are staying here until our furniture arrives when we have ten miles further to go.'

The upper part of Godolphin Road at a slightly later date, shown on a rather murky Hawke photo card. Station Road was to the left by the second cart (probably a railway delivery vehicle). My grandmother later lived in a house beyond the far one on the right – it looks as if her house had not been built when the photograph was taken. It was a good spot from which to watch the branch engines running round their trains. After a passenger train arrived, in those days of public transport integration, there would be a procession of buses coming down Station Road heading for the outlying areas.

An Edwardian view of Meneage Road, referred to as 'The Lizard Road' on the card. Except for the sprouting of lamps and poles, the scene has not greatly changed. (Anonymous, printed in Saxony.)

This anonymous card, posted in 1906, is entitled 'Helston The Moors'. It shows the Cober Valley running inland from St John's. The Moors are the rough ground appearing in the valley bottom at the left and have been a popular spot for walking and blackberrying. A noticeable feature is the raised leat which took water from the Cober to the Town Mill, one of many corn mills that once flourished on the Cober, now converted into flats. Residential development has now spread over the far hillside.

The chapel by the Cober at St John's in which John Wesley preached. It has been demolished in recent years. Wesley preached at Wendron in 1745 but not in Helston until 1755 because of the strong local opposition to him. This was overcome and the chapel established at St John's, which name Wesley used rather than Helston for some years. In 1765 Wesley was able to record, 'I preached near Helston to an exceedingly large and serious congregation. What a surprising change is wrought here also within a few years, where a Methodist Preacher could hardly go through the street, without a shower of stones.' His last visit was in 1789 (Toy, pp. 346–9). (Stengel.)

St John's Hill, where the Penzance road begins its climb out of the town. The road was then a narrow, muddy lane. Even so, it was part of the improved turnpike which bears round to the right, which about a century before replaced the more direct but precipitous track going straight ahead up the hill. Repeated widenings of the main road have swept away all the buildings except the houses at the top left and centre. The card was posted in 1909. (Photographic and Fine Arts Co., Twickenham.)

The bottom end of the Lower Green was a wasteland subject to flooding until the Corporation marked the coronation of King George V in 1911 by laying out the Coronation Lake and Park. This early view of the lake, probably by Hawke, features Edwardian boaters and a splendid model yacht.

A later view on a Judges card, probably from the inter-war years, showing the attractive setting given to the lake by the backdrop of the old town.

Section Three

PORTHLEVEN

A Valentine vignette of the harbour scene, probably

dating from the 1950s.

An interesting early card, posted in 1903, looking over the harbour towards The Lizard. As well as a few fishing luggers there are at least four two-masted trading vessels, probably topsail schooners, and the stern of a steam collier can be seen at the far left. The schooner against the outer quay is loading china clay which can be seen heaped on the quay; there are two chutes into the ship. Bay View Terrace has not yet been built under the cliff beyond the outer harbour.

This Argall card was also posted in 1903 and shows the view in the opposite direction inland over the inner harbour. There are a good many luggers but not the enormous numbers seen in some pictures when it seems a person could cross the harbour from side to side over the boats. The covered slipway of J. Bowden & Son can be seen, with a large vessel pulled out to its left. Though there was no natural harbour at Porthleven, a company promoted a scheme to create one in 1811. Completed in 1818, it was destroyed by a storm in 1824 and reopened in 1825. However, it was still unsatisfactory, and it was not until Harvey & Co. of Hayle bought it in 1855, enclosed the harbour and built the breakwater, that it became useful.

This Hawke card, posted in 1932, shows quite a number of luggers at the inner end of the harbour. Although internal combustion engines were by then being used, there is no evidence in the picture that the boats shown had been motorized. The slipway is empty, symptomatic of the decline of local shipbuilding.

A Frith card, but also bearing the imprint of H.R. Cowls, Newsagent etc., Porthleven. The viewpoint is similar to that on the previous page. Although taken forty or fifty years later, the scene beyond the harbour is remarkably unchanged. The fishing boats have altered, the wheelhouses on most of them indicating motorization. Harvey's steam crane waits on the far quay for the arrival of the next coaster.

There are a number of attractive Judges sepia postcards which must date from the immediate post-Second World War period. There is an element of posing in this scene but no doubt the participants were on hand watching activity in the harbour and only needed positioning. The view is looking west over the harbour to the early warehouse with its hoist to doors at all three levels. Above it, the Breageside road climbs the cliff. It must have been a considerable engineering feat to carve the road out of the hillside, presumably done when the harbour was created. In the foreground is the traditional clutter of wicker lobster pots and drying nets.

A Frith card showing the outer harbour in the thirties, to judge by the vehicle standing on the quay, centre left. It looks like an early pickup but has tanks on each side of the loadspace. It probably supplied fuel or water to the boats. In favourable weather conditions it was common to unload fish at this point to save time. Bay View Terrace is conspicuous in the background (compare with p. 32).

The outer harbour from a different angle in post-war times. The more modern truck bears the name of Pawlyn Bros. Ltd, Fish Merchants, Mevagissey and the catch is being loaded straight into barrels and on to the truck. The Ship Inn is at the left. (Judges.)

The harbour approach, in what must be a Hawke card, although it is unmarked. The whole fishing fleet seems to be lying off, perhaps awaiting a favourable time to sail. In this inter-war view there are two or three wheelhouses so the fleet is probably a mixture of pure sail and motorized vessels. The lifeboat house is at the centre. A lifeboat was sited at Porthleven from 1863 to 1929, during which time fifty lives were saved.

Postcards were first authorized in 1894 and until 1897 it was not permitted to write anything other than the address on the back. This Wharton card is of that type and is the oldest of these pictures of Porthleven. It shows a fleet of fishing boats putting to sea. Interestingly they do not seem to be the home fleet of luggers but some visiting yawls, perhaps foreign. The lack of Bay View Terrace is noticeable.

A Frith card from the Edwardian period showing the seine net being hauled on to the quay of the outer harbour. By this time the once-great seining industry, when huge shoals of pilchards were caught in these special nets as they came inshore, was in terminal decline. Steam trawlers were producing more attractive and more reliable catches, and the shoals disappeared, perhaps disrupted by the new methods.

Looking from the pier or breakwater towards the Institute, a very distinctive feature of the village, with its miniature Big Ben clocktower, often mistaken for a church. (Judges.)

Above the Institute is Peverell Terrace, seen here in the centre, with the Coastguard Station on the right. The village below is dominated by what is now the Methodist church. Porthleven developed as a significant settlement only after the harbour was built; as a result, it had no parish church, being part of the parish of Sithney, which it still is. Methodism was stronger in the village and the imposing Wesleyan chapel was built at the cost of £3,720 in 1883. Even so an unkind wag has rhymed, 'They built the church, upon my word, as fine as any abbey; and then they thought to cheat the Lord, and built the back part shabby.'

Looking down on the harbour from Peverell Terrace in one of Judges' early post-Second World War cards. The derelict building at the centre beyond the harbour was built to store china clay for shipment; clay was brought from the workings around Tregonning Hill, which appears as a hump on the skyline. Fortunately this interesting building has since been restored for retail and display purposes.

The long shingle beach begins east of the breakwater and runs for three miles or so to Gunwalloe Fishing Cove, encompassing the Loe Bar en route. Here Porthleven faces a destructive sea and some of the buildings shown have disappeared into it. Major defence works have been undertaken in recent years. In the distance is Trewavas Head, its old mine engine houses just discernible. (Valentine, posted in 1903.)

Further east of the breakwater is the area known as Gravesend from the time when shipwreck victims were buried there, in great contrast to this calm summer scene. Cudden Point can now be seen beyond Trewavas and, as a dim smudge on the horizon, the Land's End peninsula forming the western arm of Mount's Bay. (Judges.)

THE LOE TO POLURRIAN

A Judges study of The Loe seen from Penrose Walk

looking inland towards Helston.

A Frith view of the Loe Bar from the west. It is believed that the sea at one time ran up to Helston and that the Bar was created by tidal sweep or stormy upheaval, thereby converting The Loe into a freshwater lake cut off from the sea. It already existed in 1300 but seems to have been subject to periodic breakouts of the fresh water; these occurred less frequently as the Bar grew bigger over the years. By the nineteenth century it was necessary for Helston people to cut the Bar from time to time to prevent flooding in the town. In about 1850 miners created an adit at the western end which usually drains the lake but, because of blockage, it was necessary to cut the Bar again in 1979 and 1984.

The central part of The Loe. It is commonly called the Loe Pool but The Loe is more correct, as *loe* means pool in Cornish. It is about 1¼ miles long and 4¼ round. The Loe formed part of the largest gift ever received by the National Trust in Cornwall. Some 1,600 acres were given by the Rogers family of Penrose in 1974. Penrose lies on the right of the picture, which is looking seawards. (For more about the Pool and Bar, see Harris and Ivey, books mentioned in the Acknowledgements.)

Most of the classic shipwreck photographs, like this one, were taken by Gibson & Sons. It shows the SS *Tripolitania* aground on Loe Bar. Many sailing ships came to grief after becoming embayed in Mount's Bay. It was unusual for a steamer, but riding high in ballast, she could not make headway against a terrific gale and went aground on Boxing Day 1912. Despite efforts over nearly two years she could not be refloated and was broken up where she lay. The previous owner of the card has written information about the vessel on the back. She was 2,353 net tons, built as the *Drumgarth* at Sunderland in 1897, later became the *Lord Cromer* and was sold to Italian owners in 1911. There have been many terrible wrecks on the Bar, the worst being that of the frigate HMS *Anson* in 1807 when over 120 crew members died, an event which inspired Helstonian Henry Trengrouse to develop the rocket life-saving apparatus.

A Hawke card of the Helston end of Gunwalloe. It was posted 26 June 1930, addressed from the Halzephron Hotel, and the message reads: 'This is a heavenly little spot – 5 miles from the railway station – a sweet little white-washed hotel & very comfortable – weather is perfect.'

The Halzephron Hotel on another contemporary Hawke card, with only a modest sign over the porch to identify it. A family group lurks among the shocks in the cornfield in the foreground. My sister and brother-in-law have recently become the proprietors of the Halzephron Inn, as it now is. It is named after the nearby tall and forbidding Halzephron or Halsferran Cliffs.

A track opposite the Halzephron leads down to the eastern extremity of the long beach from Porthleven, recorded on this Hawke card as Gunwalloe Fishing Cove. Fishing from this exposed location can never have been easy, its only facility being the access ramp from the land. Guernseys were common dairy stock in Cornwall before Friesians became universal.

The church of St Winwaloe, from which Gunwalloe gets its name. It is remote from the village, beautifully situated on the shore of Church Cove. The main building is of typical local style of the fourteenth and fifteenth centuries. Unusually, the older tower is separate, built into the cliff. Surviving fragments of the rood screen are said to have been carved out of timber from the wreck in 1526 of the immensely rich Portuguese vessel *St Anthony*. St Winwaloe is believed to have come from Brittany and to have founded the church in the sixth century. (An early card, posted in 1902.)

A Hawke photograph of the All Souls' Day ceremony on the rocks at Church Cove. Though I have been able to find out little about it, the ceremony was probably introduced by Father Wason, the clergyman officiating here. The man and boy behind the lady in black are carrying flowers which were cast on the water in memory of the countless thousands who had lost their lives in the neighbouring sea. However, Father Wason's innovations were not universally welcomed: in a book published in 1909, A.G. Folliott Stokes recorded of the church: 'This little building has lately been the scene of considerable strife, owing to the ritualistic tendencies of the present incumbent. The Cornish people cling tenaciously to the simple habits and mode of worship of Christ and His disciples during the three years of His ministry and are averse to all ecclesiastical additions . . . so they have thrown the vicar's images, candlesticks and pictures into the sea.' The clothing of the lay people seems to date the picture to about 1910.

Another All Souls' Day ceremony in much less friendly conditions. The participants seem to be risking a wetting or worse. There is a display of Father Wason's unpopular candlesticks and censer.

An attractive study by Hawke of a sunny afternoon at Church Cove.

This Hawke card 'Zeppellin [*sic*] over Cornwall' shows a large airship off Church Cove with the Poldhu Hotel at the far left. Unfortunately nothing more is known about the picture.

A Peacock Brand 'Autochrome' card of the Edwardian era looking across the entrance of Church Cove to the Poldhu Hotel and the Marconi Wireless Telegraphic Station.

Penpol Picturecards published many good quality real-photo cards in the post-war period. Here is an attractive summer view of much the same scene as on p. 48, some fifty years later. The Marconi towers have long since gone.

Looking back to the church from the opposite side of Church Cove, it can be seen that erosion in the cove beyond could eventually leave the church on an island. The far cove is called Dollar Cove after a Spanish wreck of the 1780s whose legendary cargo has prompted many unsuccessful treasure hunts. (Frith.)

A last look back at Church Cove on a Valentine's real-photo card of exceptional quality, showing the uncluttered scenery of the early twentieth century. Poldhu Point is in the foreground, then Church and Dollar Coves before the Halzephron Cliffs. Cudden Point is just discernible in the distance.

On 12 December 1901 the first transatlantic wireless signal was transmitted from Poldhu to St John's, Newfoundland. Guglielmo Marconi began construction of the station in October 1900. The first two aerial systems were short-lived and were replaced by these four wooden towers in 1902. They were later renewed in tubular steel. Poldhu closed for transmission in 1922 but was used for experimental purposes until full closure in 1934. The Prince and Princess of Wales visited the station in 1903. There is a memorial to Marconi on the cliff, erected in 1937. (See Todd and Laws, pp. 157–9.) (A Meeks Own Series card, posted in 1913.)

A number of large and prominent hotels were built around the coast of Meneage in the late Victorian and Edwardian periods to cash in on the burgeoning middle-class tourist trade. This view of the Poldhu Hotel, presumably a publicity card produced by the hotel, was posted in 1924 with the message 'We are staying at this Hotel. It is lovely here.' It is now a residential home. The hump on the skyline is Tregonning Hill.

The next hotel along the Meneage coast was the Polurrian, above the cove of that name. The card was posted in 1903 when the hotel was about fourteen years old. In the early morning of 16 May 1909 it was completely gutted by fire.

The replacement Polurrian Hotel, shown on a Penpol card posted in 1952.

A contemporary Penpol card of Polurrian Cove with plenty of bathers and only two cars. Mullion Island is beyond.

Two views, fifty years apart, of Polurrian from the east. Above, this Frith card, posted in 1903, shows the original hotel and the Marconi towers. Below, a post-war Overland Views card showing the modern hotel.

MULLION TO KYNANCE

One of the magnificent carved bench-ends in the

church at Mullion, now incorporated in the lectern.

(Hawke.)

An early Frith card showing Mullion village from the Poldhu road before it began to expand over the fields in the foreground.

A little later, and new houses have appeared in the foreground as a splendid chauffeur-driven tourer approaches.

An Edwardian Frith view looking south down the street at Mullion. The basic structure remains much the same today, but the post office has crossed the street and a bank occupies the site of the shed at the right.

The seaward end of Mullion village street, looking north. Although posted in 1917, this Argall card must have been taken much earlier. Again, the buildings remain much the same but the uses have changed; on the right the cottage has gone and the adjoining shop has a modern front.

Mullion church in the early years of this century. The chequered appearance of the tower, built in about 1500, arises from the use of a mix of granite and serpentine stone. The War Memorial is now located in the near corner of the churchyard. The furthest of the thatched cottages is no longer standing. (Valentine.)

Moving back into the village from the scene above, the same cottages are in the distance. The two nearest are still there, but considerably changed in appearance, the nearest having lost its thatch. This Frith card was posted in 1912: 'We are having such a jolly time in this little place. The house is right on the edge of the cliff and it is great fun trying to do the housekeeping. A smelting hot day today.'

The Old Inn, a much-photographed feature of Mullion, located just round the far corner in the previous views. The wall and building on the left have been demolished. (An anonymous photo card, probably pre-First World War.)

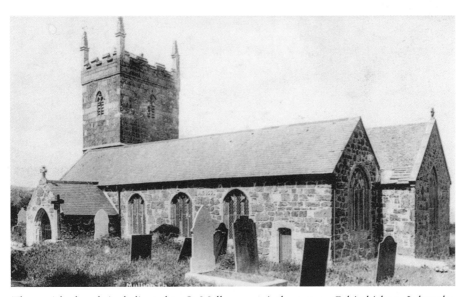

The parish church is dedicated to St Mellanus, a sixth-century Celtic bishop. It has the characteristically Cornish nave and two aisles of equal height, dating from the thirteenth century. (An anonymous but apparently early card.)

A Frith real-photo card of the attractive interior of the church, overprinted 'W. Mitchell, Supply Stores, Mullion'. Well shown here are the superb sixteenth-century oak carvings and the fine wagon-roof with original timber, reputedly with not a nail in it. The rood screen is largely reconstructed with fifteenth-century fragments.

An interesting picture in the Argall's Series of the slipway at Mullion Cove, posted in 1904. The large boats were those used for the pilchard seining, Mullion being one of the main seining centres on Mount's Bay. When the shoals of pilchards were spotted offshore in late summer, the seine boats rushed out and surrounded the shoals with their long nets. The fish were then brought to the surface, scooped out and brought by smaller boats to the cove for treatment in the cellars. The industry was in decline by the time of this picture and died out at about the time of the First World War. (See Cyril Noall, *Cornish Seines and Seiners*.)

This Frith photograph must have been taken long before it was published as a postcard. The picture shows what Mullion Cove looked like before harbour construction began in about 1887.

A much later view from the same angle, published by Overland Views in the post-war period. It shows the storm damage the inner pier had suffered, causing it to be sloped off. It has since been repaired.

A good but anonymous photo card of the harbour in the early years of the century. The piers are in good condition and a large fish cellar is in the foreground. Two or three seining boats can be made out, possibly disused. The building to the left is the lifeboat house. There was a lifeboat at Mullion from 1867 to 1908. Despite, or perhaps because of, the exposed location, only three lives were saved during that time.

An attractive Hawke view from the inter-war period photographed against the morning sun and showing detail of the piers with Mullion Island and Gull Rock beyond. The older name for the cove is Porthmellin.

Another Hawke view showing high tide in the harbour mouth, with four crabbers afloat and their pots on the quay.

This card luckily identifies its subject. It was sent by D. Paterson of Chelsea to Mr Jack Georges, Mullion Harbour: 'Dear Mr. Georges, Here is your portrait. I hope you are as fit and well, and as merry and bright, as ever.' Although printed with a postcard back it is probably Mr Paterson's own photo, does not seem to have been posted and has no date, although it is probably inter-war.

When the tide is out there is an attractive beach at Porthmellin, with a cave and other interesting rock formations, depicted here on a Peacock card.

The far end of the beach shown on an anonymous Edwardian photo card with visitors wearing the heavy and decorous clothing of the period. The feet of one man taking his ease and a young paddler can be discerned.

There is a good view back to the harbour from the cliffs to the east, shown here on a Valentine card. Prominently situated above the harbour is the Mullion Cove Hotel.

The Mullion Cove Hotel is shown in close-up on this Hawke card.

Kynance Cove can be approached along the unusual hedge-top path shown on this Frith card.

An E.A. Bragg photo card of Kynance Cove in the early years of the century. Thomas's Luncheon & Tea Rooms, on the right, is very smart, in contrast to the decaying building opposite. The stall in the centre foreground is full of serpentine carvings.

This Argall card looking up from Kynance Cove also shows the serpentine stall and the decayed buildings.

Kynance Cove from the west, with the tide fairly high. Kynance is such a great attraction partly because of the rugged coast and outlying rocks, and partly because these are composed of the multi-coloured serpentine rock of the area. The rocks have names: at the centre lies Asparagus Island (after the plant growing on it), The Bishop to its right and Lion Rock beyond on the left. (Published by H.G. Parkin, post office, Marazion.)

A Hawke photograph showing Kynance Cove from the east with a high sea running. In this photograph, taken between the wars, the nearer buildings are collapsing, but they have since been restored.

A carefully composed view of the cove by Judges showing the tide out and the buildings screened by the rocks at the right.

Other attractions of Kynance Cove are the rock formations at beach level. The Bellows on Asparagus Island consists of two holes in the rock, through which at appropriate states of tide the sea is forced in powerful jets with a loud roaring noise.

The caves in the rocks are made especially attractive by the shiny rich colours of the wet, wave-polished serpentine.

Along the high cliffs to the east of Kynance Cove, this scene emphasizes the ruggedness of the coastline, while the amount of loose rock shows how erosive forces are constantly at work.

A farewell view of Kynance by Hawke. Beyond The Bishop and Asparagus Island the setting sun touches the Atlantic horizon.

THE LIZARD

An ancient granite cross at the roadside at The

Lizard. (Frith.)

Pentreath Bay encompasses the stretch of coast between Kynance and Lizard Point, seen in the distance on this Judges card, which can be dated by the stranded ship. Curiously this vessel is not mentioned in any of the books about wrecks that I have seen nor is it mentioned on this card. Luckily I found a Hawke card of the same event which is captioned 'S.S. "Nivelle", Lizard, June 10th '23'. It is also recorded that twenty crew were rescued by the Lizard lifeboat. Perhaps the ship was refloated and did not truly become a wreck. Although Lizard Point is England's most southerly point it lacks the drama of Land's End on Cornwall's other tip. The stretch of coast from the Point to Bumble Rock past Polpeor and the lighthouse runs west to east, and it is hard to identify on the map which part is furthest south – but the Point is generally credited.

Looking back to Lizard Point from the opposite, easterly, direction across Pistol Bay (probably from the old Cornish *pystyll* for waterfall), with Polpeor Cove and lifeboat buoy in the foreground. (Valentine.)

An aerial shot by Overland Views of Polpeor Cove and the lifeboat station. The only road access to this stretch of coast comes to the little settlement of cafés and bungalows above the cliff, with very limited parking. Much more is provided by the lighthouse.

To judge by the crowds this must be a Lifeboat Day at Polpeor. The first boat was stationed here in 1859. The original house was on the slipway leading up the cliff. When the first motor lifeboat was planned in 1913 the slipway at right angles was constructed to give better launching straight into the sea. The old house was converted to a winch-house; the boat was pulled up to the house then turned on a turntable and returned to the new boathouse from the rear. The station closed in 1961 when it was replaced by the less exposed Kilcobben Cove station round the corner on the east coast. The Polpeor boats are recorded as having saved 562 lives in their century of service. (Penpol, probably early post-war.)

The war delayed the introduction of the first motor lifeboat. It was the *Frederick H. Pilley* (named after its donor) and came on station at Polpeor in 1920. This is probably the boat being dedicated and launched there in this scene from the 1920s. A bottle is being smashed against the sternpost, perhaps by Mrs Pilley. The photographer is not recorded.

A good, though anonymous, photograph of a lifeboat hitting the water at the foot of the slipway at Polpeor.

A photochrome sepia card of the view looking back to the buildings above Polpeor Cove from the cliff to the east, below the lighthouse. The lifeboat house and slipway are hidden by the point. The inlet in the foreground is Polbream Cove.

A lighthouse was first in service at The Lizard from 1619 to 1630 but failed because shipowners would not contribute to its running expenses. The present building originated in 1752 since which time it has witnessed many changes. At first, light was produced from two coal-fired beacons; oil lamps were introduced in 1812, and electricity in the form of carbon-arc lamps in 1874. Still later came filament lamps, giving the most powerful light in the British Isles. The foghorn was installed in 1874. (Frith.)

The eastern extremity of the most southerly stretch of coastline mentioned on p. 74 is marked by the distinctive Bumble Rock, well portrayed in this Hawke card.

The lighthouse seen from the east, looking across Housel Bay. Valentine's have faked a night-time scene by printing the photograph dark and adding the beam of light. (The people on the beach are something of a give-away.) The Bumble is conspicuous below the end of the beam. Only one of the lighthouse's towers now has a lantern.

A Hawke view of Housel Bay from the west, with Bass Point beyond. From the Point the coast turns sharply northward.

Lloyd's of London established a signal station at Bass Point in 1872 with a view to getting earlier and more reliable information about ship movements than was otherwise available in the pre-wireless age. Its services were available to anyone who wished to use them. I have a non-picture card which had been posted to the station on 23 February 1888 by G.H. Bate, ship and insurance broker of Fowey: 'Should the barque "Noel" of Maitland NS [Nova Scotia] from Corunna in ballast for Fowey signal at your Station please to telegraph me, and I will send you cost of same, & oblige.' After about a century improved radio communications made the station redundant. (Valentine.)

Penmenner Road leads south from The Lizard village towards the Point. It has not altered much since Frith's took this view before the First World War, which had broken out three weeks before it was posted on 27 August 1914.

One of the best-known images of The Lizard village is of early Great Western Railway buses (called cars in the caption) parked outside Hill's Hotel on The Green. The service from Helston station was one of the first regular bus services in the country and began on 15 August 1903. The two cars shown are of the early Milnes-Daimler type. Although they are probably both 20 hp chassis built in 1904 the bodies differ considerably, and the one on the right lacks its bonnet as someone peers into the engine from the far side. This is an Argall card posted in April 1914 from 'a glorious place', but probably taken soon after the introduction of the service.

A Frith card of the same vintage showing the lane to the left of Hill's Hotel depicted above. The two thatched buildings now have corrugated iron and slate roofs respectively and the picturesque atmosphere has evaporated. The sign on the shed to the left reads 'Great Western Railway, The Lizard, Parcels Receiving Office'. The post office was and is in the building at the bottom, facing the camera.

Much of The Lizard village, or Lizardtown, is straggly, windswept and not very attractive. Like most of the buildings seen here it was largely a product of the first wave of tourism in Cornwall. Looking across The Green from the north-west, the hotel (today called The Top House) is largely hidden by the older long shed in the foreground, which is now a showroom for serpentine products and other tourist wares. The character of the cars in this splendid Frith study shows it to have been taken midway between the wars when the car was first beginning to be seriously intrusive and parking started to be a problem. The name Lizard is thought to originate in the Cornish *lisarth* (high fortress). It applied originally to the Point, extended to the comparatively modern village and became applied to the whole peninsula as well, the older name for which is Meneage.

Housel Road links the village with the older settlement at Landewednack. It has not changed greatly since this Edwardian scene was captured by Frith's, when most of the houses must have been quite new. The pavement has been switched to the same side as the houses and the far farm building has become a bungalow.

The most southerly parish and church in England are at Landewednack, the modern village and the Point being in the parish as well as the older settlement around the church. This interior view of the church was posted in 1903. Note the fifteenth-century barrel roof, the large 'squint' giving visibility from south transept to chancel and at the far right the rounded Norman arch of the porch doorway. (Frith.)

Two contrasting views of Landewednack Church. Above, a Frith card posted in 1902, and below, a Valentine card probably posted soon after the Second World War. The apparent starkness of the first view is much softened by the growth of greenery in the second and it is indeed a charming spot. As at Mullion, the tower (largely fifteenth century) is built of a chequer of granite and serpentine. It holds a peal of six bells, two of them dating from the sixteenth and seventeenth centuries. The battlemented porch (thirteenth century, restored) is unusual. Like Gunwalloe, the church is dedicated to St Wynwallow. The last sermon in Cornish as a living language was preached here in 1678.

Among the most photographed scenes in the district were the picturesque cottages on the lane from the church down to Church Cove. This one is unusual. It appears to have been taken as a Christmas card by the couple standing in the doorway, who must have been the Mr and Mrs W.A. Birchall who sent it with seasonal greetings to a couple in Birkenhead. Possibly the latter were guests who had stayed here at Elm Cottage, Church Cove, the address borne on the card.

Next along from Elm Cottage was this pair of thatched cottages. The nearer has over the door 'Boat for Hire' and a name which may be R.A. Barrie. There is also a notice 'Tea Made Here' with table and chair set ready. Only the further cottage, whose notice is indecipherable, now survives. A Frith card, posted 9 August 1905, the message reads: 'our guide is a man who helped save the people off the Suffolk' (a steamer wrecked on Lizard Point on 25 September 1886).

The continuation of the lane towards Church Cove shown on a Valentine's card posted in 1904. The three-storey building, now called Marriners, is reputed to have been a 'kiddleywink' where beer was illegally brewed and sold in earlier days.

Church Cove itself, depicted on an Argall card posted in 1903. Boats used in the fishing industry and for landing trippers are pulled up on the slip. The lifeboat house on the right still exists. For a few years from 1885 a boat was stationed here to supplement the one at Polpeor but, as is apparent, launching was very difficult and only one service launch took place. The present Lizard lifeboat station is at Kilcobben, a cleft in the cliff a few hundred yards to the south, right of picture.

An E.A. Bragg sepia card of the SS *Victor* landing passengers at Church Cove. This was a popular excursion from Falmouth. The tourists took tea up the valley before returning to the ship. The *Victor* was a steam passenger tug, built in Falmouth in 1898, 153 gross tons. She engaged in the tourist trade in the summer and did tug and salvage work at other times. She attended the wrecks of the *Mohegan* and *Paris*, among others, and was sold in 1934.

Another passenger tug off Church Cove, probably the SS *Alexandra*, owned by the St Mawes Steam Tug & Passenger Co. Built in Falmouth in 1902, 73 gross tons, she was sold for war service in 1916.

CADGWITH TO COVERACK

An Argall card showing the homely tower of Ruan Minor Church.

The fishing village of Cadgwith is deservedly another great favourite with the postcard manufacturers, as this selection shows. Earliest is this Argall view from the cliffs to the north, posted in 1903. Some twenty fishing boats of varied size can be seen.

This anonymous card dating from between the wars shows the village from the south, with almost as many boats but of a changed character, motorized and no doubt used as much for tripping as fishing. Draped with nets on the slipway at the centre and to the left of the winch house are two large old open boats, which must be seine boats, relics of Cadgwith's lost pilchard fishery.

Another anonymous inter-war card, showing the mixture of nautical and domestic detail which is such an appealing feature of the village. The little shop in the shed was long-lasting, as it can also be seen in the first of the Cadgwith cards on p. 90.

An early Stengel card, looking down the valley to the village. The three-masted ship is probably the *Socoa*, which went aground in 1906 but was refloated after her cargo of cement had been jettisoned.

There was a lifeboat at Cadgwith from 1867 to 1963, during which time 388 lives were saved, a remarkable 277 of them from the White Star liner *Suevic* in 1907. This post-war Penpol card shows the *Guide of Dunkirk* lifeboat on the beach.

A picturesque and almost timeless study by Judges of boats, nets and fishermen on the beach at Cadgwith.

A popular subject in the early days of the Great Western Railway's bus service was the meeting of this latest in transport technology with the primitive form represented by the donkey cart, where the mails were passed over at Ruan Turn. AF 84 was one of the 20 hp Milnes-Daimlers introduced in 1904. (Frith.)

In the centre of Ruan Minor a horse trap and the postman with his parcels pose in front of the church, which I remember for its beautiful floral decoration at Easter time. (Peacock.)

Just north of Ruan is the hidden Poltesco Valley, leading down to Carleon Cove where there was once a large serpentine factory. The sheltered lushness of the valley, such a contrast to the windswept Goonhilly Downs above, is well captured in this anonymous photograph, posted in 1929.

A little further north, Kennack Sands is the finest beach on the peninsula. Much exploited by the car and the caravan in recent years, it looks very quiet in this anonymous card, from between the wars.

A more exciting day at Kennack. On 25 May 1925 the French steamer *Maurice Bernard* went aground in a gale on the spit which divides the beach in two. It was later refloated. (Gibson & Sons.)

The first major settlement up the coast to the north is Coverack, seen here from the south on another anonymous card of the inter-war period. The harbour lies tucked under the houses on the right.

The view from the main road approaching Coverack from the west, depicted on a Valentine card posted in 1903. Note the waterwheel, centre right, the number of thatched cottages, and the sailing trader at the quay.

The Coverack Headland was another of the large late Victorian hotels on the coast of Meneage. Seen here in original condition on a Stengel card, in July 1908 it suffered a disastrous fire, like the Pollurian Hotel the following year.

A closer view of harbour and post office, early 1900s. A trading schooner lies at the quay. Coverack is an old settlement going back at least to the early medieval period. The harbour wall must be an ancient structure, no doubt much modified and strengthened over the centuries. (Stengel.)

An anonymous post-war view posted in 1958, showing a typical harbour scene of the day. The harbour is at least as full today but the homogeneous lines of traditional boats are much less in evidence. There was a lifeboat based in a house behind the photographer when the picture was taken. The station was open from 1901 (after a series of terrible wrecks on the Manacles) to 1980, and 197 lives were saved.

St Keverne is a sizeable village lying inland and to the north of Coverack. This Argall card, posted in 1903, shows Commercial Road, the entrance to the village from the Helford direction. Most of the buildings are still there, though they have been altered. The two nearer shops have been combined into a Spar shop. The third along is still recognizable, but it has been converted into a house. Beyond it is a house bearing the inscription 'Built AD 1739 by Dorcas Pym'.

The quiet square on a sunny midday between the wars. Once a major local centre, St Keverne's importance has been reduced by improved communications. The church tower and spire were built in the fifteenth century but the spire had to be rebuilt after a lightning strike in 1770. The tower contains a ring of eight bells, inaugurated by Lord Mayor Treloar in 1907. (E.A. Sweetman, Tunbridge Wells.)

Mr Hawke climbed the church tower to get this photograph of the square looking south-west along the Helston road. It is dated September 1932. Post-war development has seen some spreading of this compact settlement into the surrounding fields.

The splendid, light interior of the church at St Keverne, seen on an Argall card posted in 1903. The pillars are of unusual multi-coloured stone. Most of the church, including the font shown, dates from the fifteenth century but the wagon roof required substantial rebuilding, as did the east end, by the Victorians. The present rood screen was added a few years after this picture.

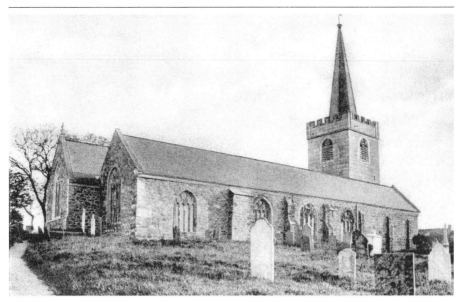

The exterior of the church at St Keverne from the north-east. The churchyard is noted for the mass graves of victims of shipwreck on the Manacles, including most of the 106 from the *Mohegan* (1898), 120 from the *John* (1855) and 104 from the transports *Dispatch* and *Primrose* (1809). A Peacock card posted in 1910.

Manacle Point and the treacherous off-shore rocks lie due east of St Keverne. One of the worst wrecks on the rocks was that of the 7,000-ton liner *Mohegan* which inexplicably hit them at full speed at 7 p.m. on 14 October 1898. She sank in the darkness in ten minutes. The Porthoustock lifeboat was called out even before the *Mohegan* hit and rescued 44 but, of the 157 on board, 106 were drowned. This Frith card shows all that remained above water.

Six months later, on 21 May 1899, the American blue-riband holder, the liner *Paris* (10,449 tons), went ashore more gently a short distance to the south on Lowlands Point in mist. All 386 passengers and 370 crew were rescued. As shown in this fine Gibson card, she was pulled clear on 12 July, the *Victor* being one of the tugs employed. She re-entered service as the *Philadelphia* and, curiously, survived another stranding in fog on the east Cornish coast in 1914.

Another fine E.A. Bragg photograph, this time of Porthoustock, a little cove just to the north of Manacle Point. The picturesque village was somewhat overshadowed by the large quarries which were developed each side of the bay from about 1896. Over the years coastal shipping took away vast tonnages of roadstone as the country's roads were tarmacadamed. There is a sailing barge at the jetty, with its massive hoppers, in the picture. The quarries, closed in 1958, are now derelict and deserted, but they dug away all the cliffside shown here behind the jetty.

The attractive centre of Porthoustock village on a Peacock card, posted in 1907. The lifeboat house to the left functioned from 1869 to 1942 and 127 lives were saved. Most of the buildings shown still exist but have undergone much change, several losing their thatch. It is an interesting exercise to stand where the photographer stood and work out what has changed.

A little to the north, Porthallow is a twin village to Porthoustock. The heart of the village is seen here, probably shortly before or after the First World War, in a card produced by The RAP Co., London. At both here and Porthoustock quarrying affected the beaches, causing a build-up of grey pebbles.

A Gibson card of the famous and terrible wreck of the *Bay of Panama*. A memorable blizzard wreaked havoc throughout the West Country on 9–10 March 1891. The *Bay of Panama*, inward bound for Dundee with jute from Calcutta, was caught in the storm and driven ashore in the middle of the night on Nare Point, north of Porthallow. She was not discovered until the morning, by which time many of the crew of forty had drowned and the survivors were freezing to death in the rigging. The coastguards from St Keverne managed to fire a line aboard and seventeen were brought ashore alive. Even then they suffered further severe hardships in the snow before they reached Falmouth overland. The *Bay of Panama* was built by Harland & Wolff in 1883 and was a four-masted, square-rigged, steel ship of 2,282 tons, described as one of the finest sailing vessels ever built. The outline of her hull can still be made out in the sea in suitable conditions.

AROUND THE HELFORD

An Argall card of Manaccan Church with its

famous fig tree growing from the tower.

This anonymous post-war card illustrates well the geography at Helford mouth. The land in the foreground runs east to Nare Point, the southern side of the entrance. In its delightful setting at the centre, St Anthony's Church looks over Gillan Creek, which leaves the main estuary just behind the Nare and runs inland to the left. Beyond the church is the Helford with Rosemullion Head marking its northern extremity and Falmouth in the distance. Dennis Head to the right of the church was the scene of one of the last stands of the Royalist forces in the Civil War.

The inner end of Gillan Creek at high tide, looking towards St Anthony's. A trading vessel lies at anchor. (Argall, posted in 1907.)

The last view was taken from Carne, which marks the head of navigation on Gillan Creek. Here is a roadside view of the hamlet taken by Hawke between the wars. It has not changed a great deal, although tidying up of the road has removed some of the picturesque quality.

A Penpol card posted in 1952, showing Carne from across Gillan Creek. The sender comments: 'I thought you would like a view of our lovely morning walk. We came right along to the mouth at low tide and waded across to our Gillan Cove.' The scene is much the same today, except that a quay has since been restored in front of the houses.

The card on this page and the one opposite are both from the very fine sepia photographs produced by E.A. Bragg of 1 Claremont Terrace, Falmouth in the Cornish Riviera Series. One of the attractions of Meneage is the striking contrast of the iron-bound coast from Halzephron to Nare Point and the open windswept expanses of Goonhilly Downs, with the placid waters of the Helford River and the sheltered greenness of its secret side valleys. This is Helford village from the east with the water of its creek just visible centre right and the Helford itself beyond. The card was posted in 1913.

From the opposite side of the valley, looking across the inner end of the village towards the lower reaches of the river. The pointed roof of the Victorian chapel can just be seen silhouetted against the river. It is now a gallery and the focus of the large car park which keeps the village mercifully free of cars. The chapel bell was salvaged from the *Bay of Panama*. The buildings have changed little over the years.

From the Victorian chapel the road drops down the eastern side of the valley into Helford village, as photographed by Hawke between the wars. The sign over the door to the left reads 'C. Mitchell Provision Dealer'. The ford over the head of the creek is out of the picture, to the right.

Although not marked, this must be another contemporary Hawke card. It shows the scene on the far side of the ford (behind the fine Austin tourer) looking north towards the river. The thatched cottages are still there.

This composite card of Manaccan was probably put together by Hawke in the inter-war years. It gives a good impression of the attractive houses which give the village its character to this day. The New Inn also remains much the same (a thatched porch has been added) and is a popular resort. The village lies in the hilly country between Carne and Helford.

The road from Manaccan to Mawgan along the south side of the Helford touches no water until in rapid succession it crosses the Gear and Mawgan Bridges at the bifurcated head of Mawgan Creek. Both are attractive old granite structures in lush valleys, with the thatched farmhouse shown here (now somewhat altered) by the second. The little open car on the poorly-made road was probably Mr Hawke's transport. The card was posted in 1923.

Mawgan-in-Meneage is not to be confused with Mawgan-in-Pydar near Newquay. This Argall card of the church of St Mawgan (a sixth-century Celtic bishop) was posted at Easter 1911. The fine church has elements from Norman to modern times but predominantly dates from the fifteenth and sixteenth centuries. The granite tower has a peal of six bells.

Argall also recorded the village street at Mawgan early this century. The scene is still readily recognizable. The tin shed has been replaced by a garage, the cottage beyond has been extended and front gardens have been enclosed. As with many of these old scenes, road surfacing and modern traffic have made perhaps the greatest impact.

West of Mawgan, the head of the Helford is found at Gweek. It was once a flourishing port for Helston and the hinterland as far as Camborne. Indeed, the name is said to come from the Roman *vicus*, indicating very ancient trading links. Silting of the river and the decline of coastal shipping left its quays deserted by all but a few pleasure craft in this early post-war view by Penpol. The quays are now occupied by a shipyard and so are inaccessible.

Two views of the head of the Helford looking towards Gweek. The picture above is from the Bragg series and bears the message 'Monday June 12:1911. By steamer from Falmouth up to Gweek on the Helford River.' It shows both quays at Gweek, one under the steep hillside on the south bank before the river branches into two on the approach to Gweek, and the other on the north branch at Gweek itself. A barge is standing off the nearer quay. The card below (anonymous, but of about the same date) shows the same Gweek Quay with a barge lying dried out and a great deal of timber stacked. This is also the quay depicted on the previous page. The twin arches of the road bridge are still there and mark the very head of navigable water.

FLORA DAY

The Midday Dance comes down Meneage Street in

the post-war era. (Penpol.)

The origins of the Furry Dance are lost in the mists of time. In about 1700 Daniel Defoe recorded the existence of the festivities as 'an ancient and curious custom'. After a shaky spell in the mid-Victorian period when it was in danger of abolition as an uncouth pagan ritual, the dance seems to have won the support of the local upper class, such as Squire Henry Rogers of Penrose, seen here leading at Lismore with the elegant Miss Tyacke of Tenderah. (Hawke, with the date 1906 pencilled on the back.)

Squire Rogers seems to have led the dance regularly before the First World War. This anonymous card at a leafy but unknown location is undated and again shows him leading. The second gentleman has been recorded as Mr A.E. Ratcliffe.

The visit of Lord Mayor Treloar on 8 May 1907 perhaps did more than any other event to put Flora Day on the map. The background to the visit is given in Section One. Here the Lord Mayor is portrayed with the Mayor (Alfred Randle Thomas) and the band. (H.D. Wootton, Redruth.)

The Lord Mayor (marked by a cross) watching the early morning dance from the steps of the Angel. The seven o'clock dance was traditionally for the servants but nowadays it is popular with those who have work to do during the day or like the informality. (E.A. Bragg.)

This Hawke card can be dated as it was posted on 27 May 1908. The dance is held on or close to 8 May, and is clearly in the tradition of festivities to welcome the spring. The particular day may have been chosen as it is the saint's day of Helston's St Michael. The dancers seem to be hurrying from a house, perhaps having been left behind as they passed through it.

The absence of dates has made it difficult for me to put the Flora Day pictures in chronological order. No doubt someone well versed in the history of costume might find it easier, as the photographs give a wonderful record of changing fashions through the years. This Hawke card and the one on the back cover must date from the First World War period. The dance was suspended for at least some of the duration, so perhaps this is just after the end of the war. Was it a time of national emotion that allowed arms round waists, now officially frowned on, or perhaps this is not a depiction of the Midday Dance?

Another Hawke card, the clothing (jackets and buttoned skirts) suggesting the early twenties. The location is probably the gardens at the bottom of the valley between Cross and Coinagehall Streets, where many pictures were taken. The linking of the word 'Flora' with the dance seems to have originated in a bogus eighteenth-century attempt to establish a classical connection for it. The name has stuck to the day, but it is now accepted that 'Furry' is correct for the dance, although Defoe wrote, 'This festival is called the "furry" and the dance "faddy".'

In the same area, Hawke has captured the leading dancers with the ladies in archetypal twenties attire. The first couple in the Midday Dance must be Helston born. Despite the risk of mistakes, for which apologies are offered in advance, I have attempted to name some of the dancers. The first couple here are Mr J. Antron Thomas and Miss Madge Cunnack.

Probably in the grounds of Lismore (a large house and grounds off Church Street), this Hawke shot gives a splendid impression of the main dance in the 'flapper' era. The second man is Dr Tom Willis; behind him is Mr H.S. Dransfield, head of the Grammar School.

Dancing in and out of the houses has always been a feature of Flora Day. In another splendidly twenties view Hawke has captured the Midday Dance emerging from The Willows, in Church Street opposite Cross Street, now local government offices. The steward is Mr Frank Cunnack and first is Mr Douglas Wearne, third Mr J.S. Hendy, fifth Mr Edward Cunnack and sixth Mr Garfield Daniel. Mr Edward Cunnack later played so great a part in the administration of the dances that he earned the sobriquet 'Mr Flora Day'.

Photographs of the dance show parts of the town not covered in Section One. Here a dance is caught by Hawke in spirited action in Cross Street, 1920s. It remains much the same today, as attractive, dignified and quiet an off-centre street as one could hope to find in an old market town.

Moving into the thirties, Hawke shows the Midday Dancers emerging from Lesley House in Lady Street under flowering wisteria. The debonair gentleman looking at the camera is my uncle Leonard Treloar and his partner the petite Miss Estelle Tresize. The gentleman behind makes rather a striking contrast.

A section of Coinagehall Street not previously featured, shown in a Judges card of uncertain date. The ladies' clothing still has a twenties air. It must have been soon afterwards that Barclays Bank rebuilt the buildings at centre. Note the detail of the stalls and vehicles. The occasion appears to be the Children's Dance.

This Judges card bears the next reference number to the card above so it was probably taken the same day. Confusingly, it was not posted until 1938. If it was the same day, the rain has started since the previous dance and the Midday Dance is emerging from the Corn Exchange into an umbrella-holding throng. The dancers can just be made out by the line of black top-hats moving towards the bottom right corner.

Another Hawke card, dated 1939. It shows the Midday Dance in the garden of Penhellis, another large house off Cross Street. The steward is Mr John James. The first couple are believed to be Mr J. Antron Thomas and Miss Latchford (?), then Mr Douglas Wearne with Miss Thomas, the third lady is Miss Phyllis Wakeham, the fourth and fifth men Messrs Hedley Thomas (my uncle by marriage) and Mr Willie Tresize.

This anonymous tinted card may be from the immediate post-war period. The Midday Dance is at the bottom of Church Street. Mr Douglas Wearne appears again as first man, behind him Mr Geoffrey Ennor (?) and Barbara Gilbert, then Mr and Mrs Jack Gilbert.

A photograph which captures the spirit of the early post-war years. The Children's Dance is coming down Meneage Street, much to the delight of at least the lady in the centre foreground. The Children's Dance was introduced in 1922 and, danced in mid-morning, has become a great feature of Flora Day. During the Second World War, only the Children's Dance was performed, keeping the spirit of the celebration alive through those worrying years. I was at school in Helston then and well remember taking part in those wartime dances. It was a memorable day indeed when VE Day coincided with Flora Day in 1945. (E.T.W. Dennis & Sons.)

Finally, an attractive but anonymous composite card which encapsulates the spirit of Flora Day, with two shots of the Midday, two of the Early and one of the Children's Dances. They must have been taken before 1958 when grey 'toppers' began to be worn. I recognize Miss Susan Simpson (whose mother has kindly helped to identify others) in the top left photograph and local readers will no doubt enjoy recognizing many more.

This last card is not of Flora Day but is put in as a puzzle. It was taken by Hawke so is probably in Helston but I cannot identify the location. The aprons and the symbols on them indicate a Masonic procession. The nearest banner bears the name Camborne. The girls' dress suggests a pre-First World War date. There seems to be an air of solemnity and gloom. What was the occasion, when and where?

Acknowledgements

As mentioned in the Introduction, this book has been illustrated entirely from old postcards. Most of these come from my own collection, which I have built up at collectors' fairs and elsewhere over the years. The exception is a collection of cards kindly lent to me by Mr Bill Mumford. They were sent by one member of his family to another who was living in the Scillies in 1902–4. In selecting the pictures I have tried not to use these I have found reproduced elsewhere, although this has not been possible in some instances where I have wished to avoid gaps in coverage.

We owe a great debt of gratitude to the photographers and publishers whose postcards have recorded so much which would otherwise be lost. Helston and district were particularly fortunate in having A.H. Hawke resident in the town. His photographs cover nearly forty years, from the early years of the century to the end of the thirties. E.A. Bragg was another Cornish photographer who produced some excellent records of the Edwardian period. When it came to shipwrecks, Gibson and Sons were supreme. Of national publishers, the greatest contribution has been made by Frith, whose carefully composed photographs cover the whole period. The Argall Series made an important input to the early years. I have named the publishers when recorded and thanks are due to them all.

Cornwall is blessed with a remarkable wealth of books on its history, social life and topography. Chief among those I found useful (and readers may enjoy) was H. Spencer Toy's monumental *History of Helston*, Oxford, 1936. Others include:

Fisher Barham, *Old Cornwall in Camera, Road Vehicles*, Glasney, 1978.
Sheila Bird, *Book of Cornish Villages*, Dovecote, 1988.
Tom Bowden, *The Cornish Coast*, in the 'In Old Photographs' series, Alan Sutton, 1994.
W. Best Harris, *The Lizard Coastline*, privately published, undated.
W.F. Ivey, Three books of 'Memories': *Old Helston & Porthleven, Old Helston, Porthleven & The Lizard Peninsula*, and *Old Helston, St. John's & Loe Pool*, privately published (?), undated.
A. Kittridge, *Passenger Steamers of the River Fal*, Twelveheads, 1988.
R. Larn & C. Carter, *Cornish Shipwrecks, The South Coast*, David & Charles, 1969.
Jill Newton, *Helston Flora Day*, Bossiney, 1978; *Helford River*, Treleage, 1979; and *Bygone Helston and The Lizard*, Phillimore, 1987.
C. Noall, *Cornish Seines and Seiners*, Bradford Barton, 1972.
A.S. Oates, *Around Helston in The Old Days*, Dyllansow Truran, reprinted 1983.
J. Pearce, *The Wesleys in Cornwall*, Bradford Barton, 1964.
N. Pevsner, *Cornwall*, 'The Buildings of England' series, Penguin, 1951.
A.G. Folliott Stokes, *From Land's End to The Lizard*, Greening, 1909.
Jean Stubbs, *100 Years Around The Lizard*, Bossiney, 1985.
A.C. Todd & P. Laws, *Industrial Archaeology of Cornwall*, David & Charles, 1972.
Various of the Tor Mark Press booklets, especially C. Noall's *Cornwall's Early Lifeboats*, 1989.
The National Trust's leaflets on the coast of Cornwall. Church guides in all the churches visited.

Finally my thanks to my sister Mrs Angela Thomas and Mrs Nancy Simpson for help with identification, and to my wife Marigold for accompanying me on site visits and for constructive help throughout the preparation of this book.

BRITAIN IN OLD PHOTOGRAPHS

To order any of these titles please telephone Littlehampton Book Services on 01903 721596

ALDERNEY

Alderney: A Second Selection, *B Bonnard*

BEDFORDSHIRE

Bedfordshire at Work, *N Lutt*

BERKSHIRE

Maidenhead, *M Hayles & D Hedges*
Around Maidenhead, *M Hayles & B Hedges*
Reading, *P Southerton*
Reading: A Second Selection, *P Southerton*
Sandhurst and Crowthorne, *K Dancy*
Around Slough, *J Hunter & K Hunter*
Around Thatcham, *P Allen*
Around Windsor, *B Hedges*

BUCKINGHAMSHIRE

Buckingham and District, *R Cook*
High Wycombe, *R Goodearl*
Around Stony Stratford, *A Lambert*

CHESHIRE

Cheshire Railways, *M Hitches*
Chester, *S Nichols*

CLWYD

Clwyd Railways, *M Hitches*

CLYDESDALE

Clydesdale, *Lesmahagow Parish Historical Association*

CORNWALL

Cornish Coast, *T Bowden*
Falmouth, *P Gilson*
Lower Fal, *P Gilson*
Around Padstow, *M McCarthy*
Around Penzance, *J Holmes*
Penzance and Newlyn, *J Holmes*
Around Truro, *A Lyne*
Upper Fal, *P Gilson*

CUMBERLAND

Cockermouth and District, *J Bernard Bradbury*
Keswick and the Central Lakes, *J Marsh*
Around Penrith, *F Boyd*
Around Whitehaven, *H Fancy*

DERBYSHIRE

Derby, *D Buxton*
Around Matlock, *D Barton*

DEVON

Colyton and Seaton, *T Gosling*
Dawlish and Teignmouth, *G Gosling*
Devon Aerodromes, *K Saunders*
Exeter, *P Thomas*
Exmouth and Budleigh Salterton, *T Gosling*
From Haldon to Mid-Dartmoor, *T Hall*
Honiton and the Otter Valley, *J Yallop*
Around Kingsbridge, *K Tanner*
Around Seaton and Sidmouth, *T Gosling*
Seaton, Axminster and Lyme Regis, *T Gosling*

DORSET

Around Blandford Forum, *B Cox*
Bournemouth, *M Colman*
Bridport and the Bride Valley, *J Burrell & S Humphries*
Dorchester, *T Gosling*
Around Gillingham, *P Crocker*

DURHAM

Darlington, *G Flynn*
Darlington: A Second Selection, *G Flynn*
Durham People, *M Richardson*
Houghton-le-Spring and Hetton-le-Hole, *K Richardson*
Houghton-le-Spring and Hetton-le-Hole:
    A Second Selection, *K Richardson*
Sunderland, *S Miller & B B Bell*
Teesdale, *D Coggins*
Teesdale: A Second Selection, *P Raine*
Weardale, *J Crosby*
Weardale: A Second Selection, *J Crosby*

DYFED

Aberystwyth and North Ceredigion,
    Dyfed Cultural Services Dept
Haverfordwest, *Dyfed Cultural Services Dept*
Upper Tywi Valley, *Dyfed Cultural Services Dept*

ESSEX

Around Grays, *B Evans*

GLOUCESTERSHIRE

Along the Avon from Stratford to Tewkesbury, *J Jeremiah*
Cheltenham: A Second Selection, *R Whiting*
Cheltenham at War, *P Gill*
Cirencester, *J Welsford*
Around Cirencester, *E Cuss & P Griffiths*
Forest, The, *D Mullin*
Gloucester, *J Voyce*
Around Gloucester, *A Sutton*
Gloucester: From the Walwin Collection, *J Voyce*
North Cotswolds, *D Viner*
Severn Vale, *A Sutton*
Stonehouse to Painswick, *A Sutton*
Stroud and the Five Valleys, *S Gardiner & L Padin*
Stroud and the Five Valleys: A Second Selection,
    S Gardiner & L Padin
Stroud's Golden Valley, *S Gardiner & L Padin*
Stroudwater and Thames & Severn Canals,
    E Cuss & S Gardiner
Stroudwater and Thames & Severn Canals: A Second
    Selection, *E Cuss & S Gardiner*
Tewkesbury and the Vale of Gloucester, *C Hilton*
Thornbury to Berkeley, *J Hudson*
Uley, Dursley and Cam, *A Sutton*
Wotton-under-Edge to Chipping Sodbury, *A Sutton*

GWYNEDD

Anglesey, *M Hitches*
Gwynedd Railways, *M Hitches*
Around Llandudno, *M Hitches*
Vale of Conwy, *M Hitches*

HAMPSHIRE

Gosport, *J Sadden*
Portsmouth, *P Rogers & D Francis*

HEREFORDSHIRE

Herefordshire, *A Sandford*

HERTFORDSHIRE

Barnet, *I Norrie*
Hitchin, *A Fleck*
St Albans, *S Mullins*
Stevenage, *M Appleton*

ISLE OF MAN

The Tourist Trophy, *B Snelling*

ISLE OF WIGHT

Newport, *D Parr*
Around Ryde, *D Parr*

JERSEY

Jersey: A Third Selection, *R Lemprière*

KENT

Bexley, *M Scott*
Broadstairs and St Peter's, *J Whyman*
Bromley, Keston and Hayes, *M Scott*
Canterbury: A Second Selection, *D Butler*
Chatham and Gillingham, *P MacDougall*
Chatham Dockyard, *P MacDougall*
Deal, *J Broady*
Early Broadstairs and St Peter's, *B Wootton*
East Kent at War, *D Collyer*
Eltham, *J Kennett*
Folkestone: A Second Selection, *A Taylor & E Rooney*
Goudhurst to Tenterden, *A Guilmant*
Gravesend, *R Hiscock*
Around Gravesham, *R Hiscock & D Grierson*
Herne Bay, *J Hawkins*
Lympne Airport, *D Collyer*
Maidstone, *I Hales*
Margate, *R Clements*
RAF Hawkinge, *R Humphreys*
RAF Manston, *RAF Manston History Club*
RAF Manston: A Second Selection,
    RAF Manston History Club
Ramsgate and Thanet Life, *D Perkins*
Romney Marsh, *E Carpenter*
Sandwich, *C Wanostrocht*
Around Tonbridge, *C Bell*
Tunbridge Wells, *M Rowlands & I Beavis*
Tunbridge Wells: A Second Selection,
    M Rowlands & I Beavis
Around Whitstable, *C Court*
Wingham, Adisham and Littlebourne, *M Crane*

LANCASHIRE

Around Barrow-in-Furness, *J Garbutt & J Marsh*
Blackpool, *C Rothwell*
Bury, *J Hudson*
Chorley and District, *J Smith*
Fleetwood, *C Rothwell*
Heywood, *J Hudson*
Around Kirkham, *C Rothwell*
Lancashire North of the Sands, *J Garbutt & J Marsh*
Around Lancaster, *S Ashworth*
Lytham St Anne's, *C Rothwell*
North Fylde, *C Rothwell*
Radcliffe, *J Hudson*
Rossendale, *B Moore & N Dunnachie*

LEICESTERSHIRE

Around Ashby-de-la-Zouch, *K Hillier*
Charnwood Forest, *I Keil, W Humphrey & D Wix*
Leicester, *D Burton*
Leicester: A Second Selection, *D Burton*
Melton Mowbray, *T Hickman*
Around Melton Mowbray, *T Hickman*
River Soar, *D Wix, P Shacklock & I Keil*
Rutland, *T Clough*
Vale of Belvoir, *T Hickman*
Around the Welland Valley, *S Mastoris*

LINCOLNSHIRE

Grimsby, *J Tierney*
Around Grimsby, *J Tierney*
Grimsby Docks, *J Tierney*
Lincoln, *D Cuppleditch*

Scunthorpe, *D Taylor*
Skegness, *W Kime*
Around Skegness, *W Kime*

LONDON

Balham and Tooting, *P Loobey*
Crystal Palace, Penge & Anerley, *M Scott*
Greenwich and Woolwich, *K Clark*
Hackney: A Second Selection, *D Mander*
Lewisham and Deptford, *J Coulter*
Lewisham and Deptford: A Second Selection, *J Coulter*
Streatham, *P Loobey*
Around Whetstone and North Finchley, *J Heathfield*
Woolwich, *B Evans*

MONMOUTHSHIRE

Chepstow and the River Wye, *A Rainsbury*
Monmouth and the River Wye, *Monmouth Museum*

NORFOLK

Great Yarmouth, *M Teun*
Norwich, *M Colman*
Wymondham and Attleborough, *P Yaxley*

NORTHAMPTONSHIRE

Around Stony Stratford, *A Lambert*

NOTTINGHAMSHIRE

Arnold and Bestwood, *M Spick*
Arnold and Bestwood: A Second Selection, *M Spick*
Changing Face of Nottingham, *G Oldfield*
Mansfield, *Old Mansfield Society*
Around Newark, *T Warner*
Nottingham: 1944–1974, *D Whitworth*
Sherwood Forest, *D Ottewell*
Victorian Nottingham, *M Payne*

OXFORDSHIRE

Around Abingdon, *P Horn*
Banburyshire, *M Barnett & S Gosling*
Burford, *A Jewell*
Around Didcot and the Hagbournes, *B Lingham*
Garsington, *M Gunther*
Around Henley-on-Thames, *S Ellis*
Oxford: The University, *J Rhodes*
Thame to Watlington, *N Hood*
Around Wallingford, *D Beasley*
Witney, *T Worley*
Around Witney, *C Mitchell*
Witney District, *T Worley*
Around Woodstock, *J Bond*

POWYS

Brecon, *Brecknock Museum*
Welshpool, *E Bredsdorff*

SHROPSHIRE

Shrewsbury, *D Trumper*
Whitchurch to Market Drayton, *M Morris*

SOMERSET

Bath, *J Hudson*
Bridgwater and the River Parrett, *R Fitzhugh*
Bristol, *D Moorcroft & N Campbell-Sharp*
Changing Face of Keynsham,
  B Lowe & M Whitehead

Chard and Ilminster, *G Gosling & F Huddy*
Crewkerne and the Ham Stone Villages,
  G Gosling & F Huddy
Around Keynsham and Saltford, *B Lowe & T Brown*
Midsomer Norton and Radstock, *C Howell*
Somerton, Ilchester and Langport, *G Gosling & F Huddy*
Taunton, *N Chipchase*
Around Taunton, *N Chipchase*
Wells, *C Howell*
Weston-Super-Mare, *S Poole*
Around Weston-Super-Mare, *S Poole*
West Somerset Villages, *K Houghton & L Thomas*

STAFFORDSHIRE

Aldridge, *J Farrow*
Bilston, *E Rees*
Black Country Transport: Aviation, *A Brew*
Around Burton upon Trent, *G Sowerby & R Farman*
Bushbury, *A Chatwin, M Mills & E Rees*
Around Cannock, *M Mills & S Belcher*
Around Leek, *R Poole*
Lichfield, *H Clayton & K Simmons*
Around Pattingham and Wombourne, *M Griffiths, P Leigh & M Mills*
Around Rugeley, *T Randall & J Anslow*
Smethwick, *J Maddison*
Stafford, *J Anslow & T Randall*
Around Stafford, *J Anslow & T Randall*
Stoke-on-Trent, *I Lawley*
Around Tamworth, *R Sulima*
Around Tettenhall and Codsall, *M Mills*
Tipton, Wednesbury and Darlaston, *R Pearson*
Walsall, *D Gilbert & M Lewis*
Wednesbury, *I Bott*
West Bromwich, *R Pearson*

SUFFOLK

Ipswich: A Second Selection, *D Kindred*
Around Ipswich, *D Kindred*
Around Mildenhall, *C Dring*
Southwold to Aldeburgh, *H Phelps*
Around Woodbridge, *H Phelps*

SURREY

Cheam and Belmont, *P Berry*
Croydon, *S Bligh*
Dorking and District, *K Harding*
Around Dorking, *A Jackson*
Around Epsom, *P Berry*
Farnham: A Second Selection, *J Parratt*
Around Haslemere and Hindhead, *T Winter & G Collyer*
Richmond, *Richmond Local History Society*
Sutton, *P Berry*

SUSSEX

Arundel and the Arun Valley, *J Godfrey*
Bishopstone and Seaford, *P Pople & P Berry*
Brighton and Hove, *J Middleton*
Brighton and Hove: A Second Selection, *J Middleton*
Around Crawley, *M Goldsmith*
Hastings, *P Haines*
Hastings: A Second Selection, *P Haines*
Around Haywards Heath, *J Middleton*
Around Heathfield, *A Gillet & B Russell*
Around Heathfield: A Second Selection,
  A Gillet & B Russell
High Weald, *B Harwood*
High Weald: A Second Selection, *B Harwood*
Horsham and District, *T Wales*

Lewes, *J Middleton*
RAF Tangmere, *A Saunders*
Around Rye, *A Dickinson*
Around Worthing, *S White*

WARWICKSHIRE

Along the Avon from Stratford to Tewkesbury, *J Jeremiah*
Bedworth, *J Burton*
Coventry, *D McGrory*
Around Coventry, *D McGrory*
Nuneaton, *S Clews & S Vaughan*
Around Royal Leamington Spa, *J Cameron*
Around Royal Leamington Spa: A Second Selection,
  J Cameron
Around Warwick, *R Booth*

WESTMORLAND

Eden Valley, *J Marsh*
Kendal, *M & P Duff*
South Westmorland Villages, *J Marsh*
Westmorland Lakes, *J Marsh*

WILTSHIRE

Around Amesbury, *P Daniels*
Chippenham and Lacock, *A Wilson & M Wilson*
Around Corsham and Box, *A Wilson & M Wilson*
Around Devizes, *D Buxton*
Around Highworth, *G Tanner*
Around Highworth and Faringdon, *G Tanner*
Around Malmesbury, *A Wilson*
Marlborough: A Second Selection, *P Colman*
Around Melksham,
  Melksham and District Historical Association
Nadder Valley, *R. Sawyer*
Salisbury, *P Saunders*
Salisbury: A Second Selection, *P Daniels*
Salisbury: A Third Selection, *P Daniels*
Around Salisbury, *P Daniels*
Swindon: A Third Selection, *The Swindon Society*
Swindon: A Fourth Selection, *The Swindon Society*
Trowbridge, *M Marshman*
Around Wilton, *P Daniels*
Around Wootton Bassett, Cricklade and Purton, *T Sharp*

WORCESTERSHIRE

Evesham to Bredon, *F Archer*
Around Malvern, *K Smith*
Around Pershore, *M Dowty*
Redditch and the Needle District, *R Saunders*
Redditch: A Second Selection, *R Saunders*
Around Tenbury Wells, *D Green*
Worcester, *M Dowty*
Around Worcester, *R Jones*
Worcester in a Day, *M Dowty*
Worcestershire at Work, *R Jones*

YORKSHIRE

Huddersfield: A Second Selection, *H Wheeler*
Huddersfield: A Third Selection, *H Wheeler*
Leeds Road and Rail, *R Vickers*
Pontefract, *R van Riel*
Scarborough, *D Coggins*
Scarborough's War Years, *R Percy*
Skipton and the Dales, *Friends of the Craven Museum*
Around Skipton-in-Craven, *Friends of the Craven Museum*
Yorkshire Wolds, *I & M Sumner*